African Angels

African Angels

Poetry for the Mind, Body and Spirit

Keenan Pendergrass

Writer's Showcase
presented by *Writer's Digest*
San Jose New York Lincoln Shanghai

African Angels
Poetry for the Mind, Body and Spirit
www.poeticsoul.com

Writer's Showcase
presented by *Writer's Digest*
an imprint of iUniverse.com, Inc.

For information address:
iUniverse.com, Inc.
5220 S 16th, Ste. 200
Lincoln, NE 68512
www.iuniverse.com

ISBN: 0-595-15060-8

Printed in the United States of America

*This book is dedicated to the memory of my grandmother Vera Pendergrass.
She taught me the true meaning of Spirit and how to trust my inner voice.*

Preface

There is a spiritual revolution taking hold in our society; A revelation that is awakening the souls of people all over the globe. This collection of poems speaks to that awakening. The concept for the project first came to mind while I was sitting in church on New Year's Eve, 1995. The premise seemed simple enough ... take the sermon each Sunday and build a poem around the message. The process was more involved... it made me listen to each sermon differently, to absorb the words and feel the emotion that they inspired. Over time I was able to internalize the message I heard and create poems that captured the essence of each message. Gradually I began writing poems about everyday life. The challenges, successes, questions and failures we all experience seemed to have different meaning for through my poetry, I was being Led By The Spirit. The veil had been pulled back and I was able to see, if only for an instant, what had been invisible. I tried to put that revelation on paper in the form of this book. I am not trying to preach, teach or condemn but rather to excite, inspire and motivate you to look at your world a little differently. All we really have is NOW, we can and should plan for tomorrow and we often lament the missed joys and opportunities of yesterday but the only thing that is certain is this moment in time. NOW! Live your life to its fullest, appreciate what you have, celebrate your journey and open yourself to all the possibilities this universe has to offer.

Preface

We are an amazing people. Whatever we believe in, whatever we focus on manifest itself into our reality.

"Ask, and it shall be given you; seek, and ye shall find; knock, and it shall be opened unto you": Matthew 7:7

Your words are the most powerful gift you own. Do you use them for good?

Reverend Freddie T. Phiphus, minister at Lincoln Heights Missionary Baptist Church in Cincinnati, Ohio was my minister for seven years and it was his sermons and his growth and his vision that inspired many of the poems that you find in this collection. One Easter Sunday he asked a question, "If your words were clothes how would you be dressed?" Would you be proud of your clothing or would you be embarrassed by what you had to wear? Would your clothes be a positive inspiration to all whom met you or would they be so negative and ugly that people had to turn away? Would they be clean, new garments shining as bright as a beacon or would they be tattered and torn rags, dirty with the stench of the gutter?… If your words were clothes how would you be dressed?"

Acknowledgements

Reverend Phiphus your growth and guidance were an inspiration; Toni your love, friendship, encouragement and support are a blessing; C. Marie you let me see the Christ in you and I will always be grateful for the lesson; Brenda thanks for putting me on the path; Denise you fed my creativity; Marlene, DeDe, Artrese and Alonda I love your spirit…you're all very special! Your energy, honesty and excitement got me back on track…Alonda, YOU are my African Angel; Kelvin you've always been my rock…your vision, and insight helped to bring my dreams to life. Mom and Dad your undying love and support have given me more confidence than you will ever know.

…Wow..Yo

Contents

African Angels

Poetry for the Mind, Body and Spirit

Keenan Pendergrass

Introduction

Poems have their own purpose, their own character, their own guiding spirit… Each poem in this collection an angel…an "African Angel" sent to comfort, protect, challenge and enlighten your soul. Consider them African Angels because they came from the spirit of my ancestors in the form of verse and rhyme. I share these poems with you in love…may they bless your soul.

Hope
_____

Poems of Hope

God's Miracles

Granny used to ask
The Lord for a miracle
Each and every day
Then thank him for
Providing it each night
When she'd pray

One day I said…
I saw nothing miraculous,
No angels from on high
She smiled
And simply turned
Her gaze toward the sky

Baby look around you
God's miracles abound
Each day is full of miracles…
There's no reason
For your frown.

The birds fly south
Right on cue
The plants are watered
By morning's dew
Watching you grow
Is miraculous to me
Don't take for granted the

Keenan Pendergrass

Wonderful things you can see

Life is a Miracle
A blessing from on high
And if you ever forget
Just turn your gaze
Toward the sky

Now I ask
The Lord for a miracle
Each and every day
Then thank him for
Providing it each night when I pray.

Prayer is just the Start

I prayed for a miracle
Just the other day
I knew the shape and form
It should take
When I wanted it to arrive
So I wouldn't have to wake
Early in the morning or
Late at night
I prayed for a miracle
And it had to be just right.

I prayed for a miracle
And scheduled the time
I sat there patiently
And told God what to do
Once my job was done
I smiled for I knew
My answer would arrive
In just a short while
I prayed for a miracle
Why am I still in denial
About the issues that haunt me
Both day and night
I try to ignore them
But find no delight
In fooling my self
Or the people I love

And that's when God spoke
From heaven above.

"…The blessings you receive
come not because you pray.
Prayer becomes a miracle
Because you work each and every day
Preparing for the miracle
To come down from on high
The miracle is hidden
In the faith you must find
The miracle is in the work
For it brings you peace of mind…"

Prayer is the beginning
Work is the key
And when you can feel the magic
What wonders you will see
As miracle follows miracle
And joy fills your heart
The two must work together
Prayer is just the start

The Scattering

Some people stay
in one city all their life
Though that doesn't necessarily reduce
pain, drama or their level of strife
For they are the anchors
Who build on a dream
Theirs is a vision
that doesn't always seem
Glamorous or
Exciting or
Inspiring at first glance

But look again and
you'll get a chance to see
the backbone of our society
Teachers, Doctors, Laborers, and more
Everyday people working to restore
The integrity we all once knew

They tow the line
They make the Grade
While some of us are Scattered
To share what we know
To champion their vision
So we all might grow

Keenan Pendergrass

From city to city
We champion a cause
Sharing that vision
Not looking for applause
Many are Scattered
Across the land
Carrying God's message
Implementing his plan
Touching the spirit
Of those that we find
To the Teachers, Doctors, Laborers ...and their kids
We bring the future by remembering the past
We hold the light
We are the Scattered
And we champion God's fight.

Everything Happens For A Reason

A verse for Ciana

Everything happens for a reason
But people only tell you that when something
Just happened that was bad
Left you sad
Searching for the reason why and
Anything that will help you dry
The tears that stream down
Your face like a river flooding its banks.
Everything happens for a reason
But that doesn't stop the pain
And you might never understand
How the loss is worth the understanding you gain
But unless you try
Whatever was taken away
Will be lost in vain
And hiding,
Trying to create a reality you can live in
Will surely drive you insane
We're all children of God
And regardless of our age
Crawling into a shell
Or throwing fits of rage
Won't make the pain go away

Everything happens for a reason
But it's up to you to find out
What that reason might be
Believe what you feel
Not what you see
Don't let anyone tell you,
Tame you, Shame you,
Blame you or Judge you
Cause they've got their own journey
To go through

All of us do
It's called LIFE and it ain't always fair
Sometimes you feel all alone
But God never puts more on you
Than you can bear
Stand on your faith
Know God is always there
Dare to dream
When all seems lost
And the dark clouds will eventually part
The pain is the start of the healing
Don't deny what you're feeling
Cause ... Everything Happens For A Reason

One Song

There is a question
That man has asked
Since the beginning of time
But no one ever stops to listen to the answer
No one wants to hold the rhythm of the Universal Rhyme
In their heart until it explodes into all the colors of the rainbow
For fear they won't survive
But you will never truly feel alive
Until the explosion rings in your ears
And you realize you are still here
Devoid of the fear that once froze you in your tracks
You now know the meaning of life
As you feel the rhythm of the Universal Rhyme
Beating where you once had a heart
Pumping energy through your veins
And radiating a light from your soul
That can't be contained
You now know your purpose
Is to learn the Rhythm of the Universal Rhyme
And share it with your fellow man
To learn the One-Song
The Uni-Verse

ONE SONG

UNIVERSE

ONE SONG

The Song of LOVE
That is the purpose of man

Passion

Passion looks like
A red hot flame
You can touch

Hold it in your hand
Feel the intensity that
Radiates from its core
Like the beauty of a rose
The vibrant colors of a rainbow
Let your passion show
Let the intensity grow
Let the universe know

Passion looks like
A red hot flame
That you can touch

It transports you
To another plane
Where spirits intertwine
And divine revelations appear
To dance the dance of joy
Effortless, Limitless, Enlightening
No more frightening
Than the beauty of a rose
The vibrant colors of a rainbow
Let your passion show

Keenan Pendergrass

Let the intensity grow
Let the universe know

Passion looks like
A red hot flame
That you can touch

Judge Not

Things are seldom as they appear
But you judge me
Based on what you see
You judge me
Instead of judging
yourself in relationship to who
I appear to be

It doesn't matter
who I am
what I have
where I'm from
Come Clean
You've got issues too
Judge Not
Lest ye be Judged
Accept Me
Love Me
Unconditionally
Even if you don't like me
Expose me
To the love in your heart
And maybe I will start to understand

Things are seldom as they appear
Let go of the fear
For your angel may come to you

in many forms
Judge Not
What you see
Lest you throw away an opportunity
To follow your destiny to greatness

Things are seldom as they appear
There's only ONE Judge
And he's in heaven above
Love is the key

It's not your job to Judge me
Judge yourself in relationship to who
I appear to be
Expose me
To the love in your heart
And maybe I will start to understand

Keep Smiling

Your smile is contagious
Your spirit divine
And each time you touch someone
They'll find it hard to confine
The smile they feel building inside
It starts as a tingle
Deep in the chest
Like a giant wave
Just about to crest
Then on to their eyes
A twinkle you'll see
Bright as sunshine
Bouncing of morning's dew
Your smile is God's Spirit
Shining through

Keep Smiling

Give In To the Spirit

I can't give you
More than I have
My energy
Will not bring you peace
Increase
Your level of happiness
Or your ability
To survive
Thrive
In a world full of chaos
For I am only a guide
Sent to show you the way
To find your light
Your birth right
But it's cancelled by ego
By pride
Give into the spirit
And you will find the doors
That open unto heaven
Right here on earth
It's worth
The price of admission
Though you cannot describe
The wonderful things
You will see
Give into the spirit
And all will be yours

Peace

I stand here knee deep in chaos
Another storm on the horizon
Another challenge about to unfold
Searching for serenity where none exists
The winds of change have no pity for me
The rain created by the storm won't set me free
Or cleanse my soul
The peace I seek is centuries old
The peace I seek lives inside the storm
Where the wind is silent
Where it's calm and warm
With chaos pressing at every pore
The peace of knowing guards the door
Like soldiers protecting their queen in times of war
Ready to lay down their lives
Before she is placed in harm's way
And so it is inside every storm
Where order rules the day
And chaos is held at bay
Your peace
Your serenity
Is but a heartbeat away
Inside the storm
Inside your soul
Search not without but within
And begin your journey to peace

The Meaning of Life

I thought I had met her once or twice
That special woman in my life
But something always told me…no
Explaining farther I must go
To find the sights yet unseen

Of Life… Of Happiness …Of Love

So I walked until nothing seemed the same
And as in my heart I always knew
A look… A touch…A silent glance
And in that instant
All about me started to dance
To the unheard melody

Of Life… Of Happiness …Of Love

And yet you're cautious
You try not to show the feelings that you've found
You close your eyes
And start to pray
Hoping that you have fulfilled the dream

Of Life… Of Happiness …Of Love

The Reality That Is You

How long can I run from myself
And hide in the shadows of my accomplishments

How long can I avoid the reality that is me
By helping you fight your demons and dragons

How far can I go without getting caught
Not for what I did
But rather what I didn't do
Winning at all costs
Often means selling your soul
To gain something you already had
And chose to give away

Why would you look at your life
Through someone else's eyes
And not appreciate the masquerade
The Disguise
That cannot be seen as lies outside the fortress
That is your very existence
Resistance is futile
And yet we all try
Can you tell me why…
I don't understand why…

Why do we make life so complex
Why do we complicate the simplest of things

Keenan Pendergrass

Why do we exchange love, honor and integrity
For houses, cars and diamond rings
Expecting to get it back
Along with the joy
We threw away
Just to say we made it to a mountaintop
Someone else defined
As your ultimate goal
Hold fast to YOUR dreams
And don't let go
Show the world
The only way to happiness
Is to know what You want

When you can answer
That one question
When you can define
That one thing
Your spirit will smile
And your heart will sing with joy
What is it you really want
What is it
Do you know
Do you want to
Or will you continue running from yourself
Hiding in the shadows of your accomplishments
Avoiding the reality that is YOU

Growth

Poems of Growth

Spiritual Beings

Spiritual Beings in human form
Free choice is our gift
We don't have to conform
To the lessons learned by others
Or the struggles they perceive
Their failures are their own
And all too often they choose to leave
Before they to see the light

Spiritual Beings
Bound only by the mind
The answers lay at your feet
If only you can find
The questions that must be asked
And the trust to accept them as true
The secrets of the universe
Will open unto you

Spiritual Beings in human form
We are all in lesson
Trying to endure storm after storm
And though they can be our teacher
Though the storms help us understand
They also challenge our faith
They can hide the Promised Land

But if you choose to endure
If you choose to grow
Someone will see your light
And want to find their own
Someone will choose to fight
Because of how you've grown
Someone will stand
Against their storm
Because they see your spirit
Not you're human form

Inside of You

There is a light inside of you
A passion that the world should see
But if you keep it hidden
If you don't allow it to glow
Then you'll find it hard to feed your spirit
You'll find it hard to grow

Your passion
Can warm people's heart
On days the sun don't shine

And be their guiding light
A way out of the wilderness
When they're walking around blind

Your passion
Can be a source of strength
To those who have lost their way

And give them life
A sense of hope
Even on their worst day

There is a light inside of you
A passion that the world should see
But if you keep it hidden
If you don't allow your light to glow

Keenan Pendergrass

You'll find it hard to feed your spirit
You'll find it impossible to grow

With Much Love

I saw your problems
But I couldn't see mine
I saw your shortcomings
And felt the need to say…

With Much Love
I offer you My Insight
Why won't you accept it as true

I saw your drama
But my issues were unclear
I saw your heartache
And felt the need to say…

With Much Love
I offer you My Solutions
Why won't you accept them as true

I saw your problems
And began to wonder why
You pushed me away
Like so many before
Couldn't you accept the truth
If not, it's time for me to hit the door

But something you said
Made me freeze

…I don't need you to save me
Won't you save yourself
Please

I saw your problems
So I wouldn't have to look my own
Now I'm dealing with my issues
And I feel I've finally grown
With Much Love
I offer you My Heart

What you see in others
Is a reflection of yourself
Although you can't always
Help someone see their own pain
If you look inside
Your search won't be in vain

Deal with your own issues
And as you grow
Others will follow your lead
In search of the peace
You now know

With Much Love
I now can see
The only problems I recognize
Are also inside of me

With Much Love
I honor you
Right where you are

The Lesson Learned

You are the teacher
…And the student

The creator
…And the creation

The lesson learned is deep within
Ask a question and you begin
Your quest…A journey
To a place yet unseen
Traveling on a road
Enveloped in darkness
But you know you've been there before
You only need the faith
To open up the door
And look inside

There you will find
The lantern
Lighting your path
And peace of mind
A knowing exists
But you must believe
For you cannot see
Nor can you retrieve
The piece of the puzzle
That makes it all clear

Without understanding
That you are the key
And nothing outside you
Can set you free

You learn from yourself
And create what you need
No question goes unanswered
But you must heed
The response that is given
Both pleasure and pain
Act as a catalyst
That help you to gain
The knowledge you seek
The questions you couldn't find
The faith that you questioned
And a spiritual frame of mind

You are the teacher
…And the student

The creator
…And the creation

The lesson learned
Is deep within
Ask a question
Let your journey begin.

It Ain't About The Pain

O.K., I'll admit it
Sometimes I'm wrong
Sometimes I cause you pain
But there's absolutely nothing
I can do about something that has
Already happened to you
It ain't about the pain
It ain't about what's wrong with me
It is about your ability to grow
In spite of the pain you may feel
It's about God
It's about faith
And whether you can sustain
Your focus
When the world is crumbling
At your feet
It's all an illusion
A blessing somehow disguised
In the form of a disaster
Or some other devastating pain
That causes your eyes to water
And your heart to weep
until you realize
It ain't about the pain
It ain't about what's wrong with me
It is about your ability to grow
In spite of the pain you may feel

Keenan Pendergrass

It's about God
It's about faith
It's about understanding what's real
LOVE
LIFE
GOD
Everything else can be replaced

It's Time

After all the stories
Of all the lessons learned through time
Why do we pretend perfect
Is where everyone begins
The moment you leave
Your parent's sight
You start to fight
For your place in this world.

You may leave them
They may leave you
Maybe they will always be there
To see you through
The challenges that are our life
And the occasional jackknife
On the highway to heaven
Or hell
The bell tolls for us all
We seek perfection but will always fall short
For no thing is perfect
And only God can make you pure
Are you so sure that throwing
Rocks at glass houses does anything
To cure your insecurity.

After all the stories
Of all the lessons learned through time

Why do we make the same mistakes
Everyone wakes from their dream
Only to realize they're living a nightmare
Yet very few dare to follow their heart
Trust their spirit
Become a part of the revolution
That always exists
Very few know what it means
To be that free
Malcolm, Martin, and Marcus Garvey
All followed their spirit
They broke the veil

They allowed the light of the Master
To shine in them
That others might see
If only for a second
What it meant to be truly free

After all the stories
Of all the lessons learned through time
Stop pretending you're drifting on a dream
Or living in a nursery rhyme
It's time to grow up
Go up to the front of the line
And lead the way
It's time to stop being afraid
Of the light of day
It's time to listen to the lessons
To learn from the past
Move into the future
On the shoulders of those who came before

African Angels

And opened a door
We could not even see
They taught us all
What it really meant to be free

It's Time
It's Your Time

I Turned My Back On You

No matter how hard I run
You're always there

No matter how deep I bury my head
You're always looking me straight in the eye

No matter how high I climb
You always get there first

No matter how scared I become
You always try to make it just a little bit worse

But no matter how hard you try
I DOUBT myself no more

See every time that you were there
God was there too
And once I learned to turn around
To look at him
I turned my back on YOU
NOT GOD

The One Truth

I stand on the abyss of freedom
Trying to decide if my mind
Can handle the truth
Despite my superior intellect
Time and again I seem to win the battle
But loose the war
My soul is slipping
Through my very fingers
While I stand on the abyss of freedom
Trying to decide if my mind
Can handle the truth

Inches separate me from my true destiny
But the potential of an infinite fall
And my inability to call the Master's name freezes my feet
I stand incomplete on the abyss of freedom
Trying to decide if my mind
Can handle the truth

My reality is but an illusion
I designed to confine my mind
Inside the perimeter of physical form
Comfortable but incomplete
Safe but never secure
I hear freedom calling my name
Luring me closer to the abyss
Like the Siren's song of old

And I hesitate to decide
If my mind can handle the truth

Am I supposed to protect my mind from
The Truth…..My Mind
THE TRUTH…MY MIND
My Mind IS The Truth
My Mind CREATES The Truth
My Mind has already Experienced The Truth…ALL TRUTH

And I realized the ONE TRUTH
There is no abyss except in my mind
And light began to shine
For I finally realized I was already FREE

Dance With Your Spirit

Don't run from yourself
There's no place to hide
Don't lie to yourself
The man in the mirror already knows
The secrets and frustrations that are a part of your life
Don't you think it's time to be real

Accept life for what it is
The good
And the bad
The joy
And the pain
One without the other would drive us all insane

There's no music without silence
No light without dark
Stark contrasts provide the variety we need
To live
To learn
To grow
Know that you are a child of God
And how you live your life
Is a choice for you to make
Won't you take a chance
Dance with your spirit
Follow your heart
Learn the secrets you hold inside

And you will no longer be denied
The happiness you seek

Sometimes you have to go down
To get up
Sometimes you have to lose
In order to win
Begin your journey
By revealing the truth you now know to yourself
And the light of the universe
Will protect you

Trust

Poems of Trust

I Am

I am the Light
That leads your way

I am the Love
You feel each day

I am the Spirit
That carries your load

I'm the calm you feel
When you want to explode

I ran to your defense
And stood at your back
Fighting off enemies
As they attacked
Picking you up
Each time you'd fall
Even when you thought
No one was there
I was waiting, listening
In case you might call

I am the God
That lives within

I am the Angel
That heaven's chose to send

I am the Love
That will always be

I am a part of you
And you're a part of me.

I Am
We Are
We will Always Be…ONE.

Before You Were Born

God ordered your steps
Before you were born
Knowing there would be days
You'd have indecision
Days you'd be torn
Between where you wanted to be
And where He needed you to be

Free to choose
We often take the most difficult path
But it's not his wrath
We encounter when things don't go our way
But rather the chaos
Of an unsaved world
God ordered your steps
And whether you're a Man,
Woman, Boy or Girl
The choice is yours to make
Lessons await
On either path
Trouble may pop up at any turn
but if you follow God's plan
You will learn
The meaning of faith
No valley sinks to low
For the river of life
Will always flow into your heart

No desert exists
God can't see you through
He ordered your steps
Laid out a plan
Then gave you the choice
To grab his hand
Or wander off on your own

God ordered your steps
Before you were born
Knowing there would be days
You'd have indecision
Days you'd be torn
Between where you wanted to be
And where He needed you to be
The choice is up to you

God's New Thing

God does a New Thing
With each breath that we take
Every step, every blink,
Every thought that we think
A New Thing
A masterpiece that doesn't hang on a wall
Or sit on a stand
It's a blessing to all
A New Thing
That we often see as the same
But every time our heart beats
We should stand and proclaim
God's New Thing
Not each year,
Or each month
Or each day
God does a New Thing
Each second that we stay
On this earth
Protected by his love
An amazing new thing
Bright as the moon and stars
In heaven above

Guided by his Spirit
Oh, can't you see
We're one in the Body of Christ

Part of heaven's jubilee
Blessed by HIS love
There's much work to do
We're God's New Thing
Let his spirit shine through

God does a New Thing
With each breath that we take
Every step, every blink,
Every thought that we think

Celebrate God's New Thing

Face Your Demons

I look to the hills
But find no comfort
I look to the hills
The high places
But find no peace
I look to the hills
The high and mighty people
But find no joy
I look to the hills
The high ideals and concepts
But find no salvation
I look to the hills
From whence cometh my help
It cometh from the LORD.
It's not about color
It's not about race
Face your demons
Fight them 'til the death
Or they will be the legacy
You leave your kids - Our kids
Hate , Fear, Intolerance
The answer doesn't have to be perfectly clear
As long as you believe there's a better way
A better day
When we will see the light of God
In other's heart
That's when the demons start to run

Keenan Pendergrass

The victory's already won
Won't you accept it
Won't you receive your blessings
I look to the hills
But find no comfort
I look to the hills
The high places
But find no peace
I look to the hills
The high and mighty people
But find no joy

I look to the hills
The high ideals and concepts
But find no salvation
I look to the hills
From whence cometh my help
It cometh from the LORD

Trusting God

The key to me
Is trusting my God
Feeling the truth flow through my veins
And knowing that although I command the reins
The direction is not mine to choose
You don't lose control if you give it to God
You gain power
And no matter how odd that may seem
No dream can provide a stranger riddle
Than
What is the key to Me
And no human can provide a better answer
Than
Trusting God

Let Go

To gain control
You've got to let go
There's no way
You can understand all the possibilities
If you only believe that two exist
Yours and mine are easy to find
But you have to suspend what you know
To see the truth
If square pegs don't fit round holes
Why are we so comfortable right now
How can you believe you control anything
When everything is a blur
And the only thing you know to be true
Is that you are in control
Let it go
If you want to know
The true meaning of control
And take charge of your destiny
Search for reality inside your illusions
See your life as you want it to be
If you hope to see the end of the rainbow
Find your pot of gold
Hold not to the reality of today
But rather your vision for tomorrow
Fighting for control is the illusion
That stole your peace
Increased the drama

African Angels

And sent your life spinning
Winning control gains you nothing
It's time to let go

All I need to know

I don't know you
And yet I do
We just met
And yet
I let you in
Allowed you to turn me inside out
And see my soul
Dance with my spirit
And hold my sensitivity
In your hand
I don't know you
And yet I do
We just met
And yet
I feel safe
Your voice comforts me
Excites me, ignites me…
I feel your strength

I don't know you
And yet I do
We just met
And yet
I can't get you out of my mind
Your gaze surrounds me
Engulfs me, inspires me
And I realized
I know all I need to know

Love

Poems of Love

Lighting In A Bottle
Blessed Union
Love Is…Everything
Your Eyes
Until Now
True Love
Holding You
My Touch, A Look And Love
My Paradise
Love Unconditional
Our Love
Everything You Thought You'd Never Do

Lighting In A Bottle

Lighting in a Bottle
Would be frightening to most
More powerful than one could hope to contain
With a potential for pain unparalleled
Yet flowing freely between two people
Happily held in the hearts
Of a man and a woman
Lighting in a bottle
Is what we all hope to find
We stake our claim
And dig in our mine
Like 49'ers of old
Searching for gold in the dark
A stark contrast to the reality we seek
Most fall to their knees weak
Unable to handle the prize
They hold so dear
And instead of joy
When we finally find love
When we finally find that Lighting in a Bottle
All you sense …
Is the fear in our heart
Only a precious few
Follow the feeling
Only the adventurous
Know the flow of lighting
The flow of love

Can be healing
Revealing secrets
Only two connected hearts can share
Lighting in a Bottle
Can be yours if you dare
To believe in the dream
And allow the thunder
To drown out the screams of fear
Only Lighting can bring

Blessed Union of Souls

I open my heart to you
And trust the magic we have created
Elated I allow my soul to sing
The ancient song of a blessed union
Remembering words many believe
No longer exists
You kissed my very essence
Released my spirit
Just as the kiss of the sun
Releases the fragrance of a rose
I respond to your touch
And recognize such joy
Is a blessing to behold
I've been told
Such love is a dream come true
A Blessed Union of Souls
A gift from God
I only know
Nothing on earth
Compares to you
The love I feel
Has allowed me to reveal
My true self
And accept you as you are
At this very moment
For no other exists
You've kissed my very essence

Keenan Pendergrass

And taught me the ancient song
Of a Blessed Union of Souls
Helped me remember words
Many believe no longer exist
And the bliss
Of being in love

Love Is ...Everything

If I could read your mind what would be revealed
What I want to know is how to make you feel
Like the love I've got to share is all you'll ever need
Whether you lead...Follow...Or we walk side by side
Don't hide what you feel
Don't hide your love

I know you've waited all your life
For the one love that would sweep you off you feet
Touch your very soul and make you feel complete
Allow you to exhale and let all the pain go
I'm here for you baby
And I want you to know I'm not going anywhere...

'Cause
Love is more than fantasy...
When the fantasy is real
Love is more than happiness...
When happiness can't explain how you really feel
Love is more than life...
When love is life itself

It's worth the pain
That's always a heart beat away
It's worth the magic
We search for each and every day
It's the melody soft and sweet

That floats from heart to ear
It's Love …And Love is worth the climb
No matter how far you might fall
Love is life's great adventure
And I can't help but to follow the Siren's call

'Cause…
Love is more than fantasy
When the fantasy is real…
Love is more than happiness
When happiness can't explain how you really feel
Love is more than life
When love is life itself

Love is …EVERYTHING

Your Eyes

Your eyes became my island
And I was captivated by the spirit
Of your regal style
I was intrigued by the beauty
Behind your knowing smile

Your eyes became my island
And I was amazed by the trust
The confidence you had
That I could keep you safe
And would never leave you sad

Your eyes became my island
And I felt a connection growing stronger
As each moment passed
So did the fear
This was a beginning
With no end in sight
This was that perfect moment
When everything felt just right

Your eyes became my island
And I was drawn to the fire
Though the danger was apparent
Your warmth fueled my desire
I could not turn away
My love is yours forever and one day

Your eyes became my island
And I was captivated by your style
I was intrigued by the beauty
Of your heavenly smile

I knew without knowing
That we were meant to be
I knew without knowing
And that knowledge set me free

Until Now

I can say
I've been touched
But not necessarily inspired
Until now

I've been appreciated
But not necessarily understood
Until now

I've been interested
But not necessarily captivated
Until now

Now, my creativity is overflowing
My passion shared
My excitement encouraged
And my honesty returned

I can say
I've been seen
But not necessarily for who I am
Until now

Now I know the meaning of Love

True Love

My soul felt heavy
My spirit felt denied
I thought I'd found love
But instead it was pride
The look was perfect
The appearance just right
The physical attraction
Created sparks
Morning, Noon and Night
But when it was quiet
I felt all alone
When I needed a friend
I found I was on my own
What I wanted
Was not what I had
I appeared to be happy
In reality I was really very sad

I'm searching for a love
That is true
A love that makes
My soul feel light
And my spirit seem to fly
A love that makes
My heart skip a beat
And everyone wonder why
I can't stop smiling

Even when things seem to go wrong
A love that is bigger
Than the challenges that we face
The problems that arise
The temptations we fight
In their perfect disguise

I'm searching for a love
That is true
A love that is effortless
A connection unmistakable
A feeling unimaginable
I am searching for love…
Real love…True Love…
I am searching for ….YOU

Holding You

*I don't know what
I'm running from
Or what I'm running to
I only know
There is a feeling
When I'm holding you
That I want to feel again
How long has it been
Days
Weeks
Seems like years
As my fears
Float to the surface
And I battle them
One by one
Remember the fun
We had just walking through the park
Moonlit nights
Romantic strolls
Now lonely reminders
Of missing you
And although that's true
I smile
For those thoughts
Warm my heart
They're a part
Of the joy I feel*

African Angels

That hold the sadness at bay
I focus on the smiles
Each and every day
Thanks for the memories
Both old and new
I can't wait till the next time
I'm holding you.

My Touch, A Look and Love

Sometimes I just can't find the words
But I've learned to try

And sometimes I think the words
Express what I feel
But your eyes don't lie

My words betray me
Leave you wanting more
Hoping
Wishing
Longing for a man who can adore
The beauty you have inside
And join you on your lonely paradise
A man to fan your fire
Drink you
Nourish you
And feed your desire

I'm aware of your passion
Bright as the colors of a rainbow
They overflow onto your canvas
Red, Purple, Yellow
You must know
Your beauty is alive
And I can see your magic
I can feel the moment

African Angels

I can see the colors in your eyes
Let me paint it for you
Starting with Purple
Gold, Blue

And then you purr
You respond to my touch
The way I look into your eye
And explore your spirit until your mesmerized
You purr because my silence says it all
So when I can't find the words
To reveal the beauty I see
I use my Touch… A Look …And Love
To reflect your beauty in me

My Paradise

Hold me in your arms
Until I feel your strength

Nourish me with your passion
Until I am warmed by your flame

Caress me with your silence
Until serenity is all I feel

Seduce me with your spirit
Until my body floats among the stars
And my paradise will be with you

Love Unconditionally

Traditionally to
Love unconditionally
Comes at a cost
I get to tell you what I see
Who I think you should be
And be with
Mentally to
Love unconditionally
Can take its toll
If you're told how to live your life
It cuts like a knife
And the wound is always there
Emotionally to
Love unconditionally
Can be your lifeline
In a sea full of sharks
To pull you out
Or pull you under
Sometimes I wonder
Isn't it best to just pause…Cause
To love unconditionally
Should be without cost
And the toll should be totally free
The line that you find
Should hold you up
Not pull you down
Even if it's done unintentionally

Keenan Pendergrass

Do you feel it's your right because
You love me unconditionally
Tell me what I need to hear
Not what you need to say
Save that for another day
Tell me that you love me
Not the person you hope I'll be
Tell me that you love ME
Not the person I pretend to be
TELL ME THAT YOU LOVE ME
TOTALLY
ABSOLUTELY
UNCONDITIONALLY

Our Love Is All The Poetry You Need

You may say no one has ever
Written you poetry
But our love
Is all the poetry you'll ever need
Listen to the rhythm
Of my heart
Feel the beat of my drum
Let me strum
Your chords of love
With a poetic pace
As we float
To a magical place
Filled with the fragrance
Of incense
And lit by candles
Romantic and dim
My love is all the poetry
You'll ever need
My hand in the small of your back
Not to attract attention
But simply to let you know
I'm always there
I'll always care
And enjoy the sight of you
The little things you do
Make my passion flow
Even the slightest kiss

Keenan Pendergrass

Makes me erupt like a volcano
Overflow onto your heart
We're apart of the same story
The same rhyme
Our love is the most beautiful poetry
Flowing perpetually
And yet frozen in time
You say no one has ever
Written you poetry
But our love is all the poetry
You will ever need

Everything You Never Thought You'd Do

*I no longer search for
The soul mate
I now know exists
With one kiss
Fate will deliver her
To my door again
But I can only win
Her heart if mine is pure
Not in spirit
But in truth
Ready to love
And be loved
Ready to let my guard down
Even wear a thorny crown
If that is what
I must do
Love is seldom defined
By what you did
But rather what you didn't do
Prepare yourself
For the one love that is true
By doing everything
You thought you'd never do.*

Inspiration

Poems of Inspiration

The PoeTTree

I stand beneath
The PoeTTree
And wait for the verse
To drop on me
Like apples
That fall from the vine
Sweet, juicy
They taste divine

I stand beneath
The PoeTTree
And thank God
For the words
That comfort me
Like shade
That provides safe haven
From summer's heat
You'll find comfort
Beneath the PoeTTree
If you take a seat

I stand beneath
The PoeTTree
But if I climb
I can see
All the things
That were meant to be

All the things
That feed the PoeTTree

Hope, Joy, Sadness, Grief
Love, Life and Death

From the Songs of Solomon
To Shakespeare's MacBeth
From Langston Hughes
To the sweet breath
Drawn by Nikki Giovanni
They share their wisdom
So all might know
Why I stand beneath
The PoeTTree
And marvel at the things
Revealed to me
Listen and learn
For it's time to grow
Stand beneath the PoeTTree
And you too will know
All the secrets of
Space and time
The healing magic
Of verse and rhyme
I'm standing beneath
The PoeTTree
And I'd be honored
If you would join me!

A Gift From God

Passion is a gift
Given at birth
And it's worth
Fortune, Fame and so much more
Passion is the key
To open any door

It flows from your lips
Your fingertips
Mysterious like a rose
Blooming in the springtime
Glorious as a setting sun

Passion defines you
Reminds you
Of the things you can't do without
It excites
Ignites you
Passion makes you dance and shout

Passion
When you and the Universe are one

Passion
Bright and radiant as the noonday sun

Passion
A gift from God

Keenan Pendergrass

The Life of a Poet...An Artist

Taking letters and words
And placing them in sometimes intimate situations

Turning a relatively innocent thought
Into heart shattering revelations

Power in a most subtle form
This is the life of a poet...an artist

A blank sheet of paper
Turned into a source of joy or pain

Painting pictures with words
As powerful as a speeding train

Manipulating thoughts as few others can do
This is the life of a poet...an artist

A determination known to few
A dedication that can only be classified as true
A talent seldom rewarded
A potential often untapped

This is the life of a poet...an artist
This is the challenge of a poet...an artist
This is the passion that guides a poet...an artist
And A Poet....An Artist lives inside of you

Embrace Your Spirit

You are God
And I am too
The love we share
Will see us through
The challenges that threaten
Each perfect day
No more than illusions
They are none the less real
We give them life
And permission to steal
Each divine moment
That is ours by grace
The choice is up to you

The life that you lead
The love you find

The path that you walk
Your frame of mind

The friends you make
The peace you feel

The battles you fight
Both imagined and real

You are God
And I am too
The love we share
Will see us through
The challenges that threaten
Each perfect day
Embrace your spirit
And what it has to say
Embrace your Spirit

The Written Word

There is a passion
That I must share
It's for the written word...

Some people find it hard to bare
The feelings they hold so dear
But for each poet
Who paints a portrait with words
I must stand and applaud

Langston Hughes
Dickens
Poe
And the amazing Maya Angelou
All share their vision
All bare their soul
And reveal their magic for the world to behold

Words make us laugh
And make us cry
Words make us feel
When we want to deny
Pain, Sorrow, Joy or Fear
Spoken words we don't always here
But written words tear at our heart
And cause emotions to be stirred

Keenan Pendergrass

We all have a passion
A talent
A gift
Mine just happens to be
The written word.

What's yours

Inspiration

Did you know
Inspiration looks like
The face of GOD
Warm
Loving
Healing
It creates a feeling
Unlike you've ever felt before
And opens a door
You didn't even know could exist

Did you know
Inspiration feels like
The face of GOD
Warm
Loving
Healing
You find yourself kneeling
Tears of joy
Bursting from your eyes
You cant disguise
Inspiration
It's the child of revelations
Old and new
The face of GOD
Revealed to you
Through the clouds in the sky

The laughter of children passing by
The beauty of a bird perched on a tree
Any believer can see
The face of GOD
Warm
Loving
Healing
And experience a feeling
Unlike you've ever known before…
Inspiration

Finish

We often choose the path
Of least resistance
Then complain of things left undone

We choose to walk away
In times of trouble
Then ask why the battle wasn't won

We choose to pass responsibility to another
Then unashamed
Seek to share their reward

We often choose to Quit
Feeling the price is too high
Then ask someone else to fight our fight
Because we no longer hold a sword

The way of the World is to Quit
The way of God is to Finish

Some people are born to teach
Others meant to lead
But we're each responsible for spreading
God word in a World full of greed

There's always another mountain
Just beyond the valley below

But those who loose their faith
Quit before they are able to grow

When you Finish
You find a new source of power
Waiting just beyond that valley
Just over the next peak
The power of God is for those who Finish
And we must help save those who are weak

The way of the World is to Quit
The way of God is to Finish

Free

Know that you are perfect
Just the way you are
Don't change for anyone
But you
Everyone has a different perspective
Of what is true
What is real
But you have to feel the love in your heart
Start to see the beauty
In your walk
Recognize your voice
As the voice of God
When you open your mouth to talk
Your beauty is there for all the world to see
But only you can set it free
Be yourself
Accept who you are
Know that you are perfect
In every way
And when you reveal your perfection
The light exposes challenges you no longer need
You've been freed
To enjoy your journey
And the challenges yet to come
Free to be yourself
Free to accept who you are
Free to enjoy your perfection

Keenan Pendergrass

> *And travel as far as your dreams will take you*
> *Know that you are perfect*
> *Just the way you are*
> *Don't change for anyone*
> *But you*

The Light

We all have a Light deep within
Grounded in the Spirit
God is able to send his blessings
In word and deed
The hurt you see comes from our need
To hide the Light which comes from above
You cannot say your Light is directed in love
Then decide which Truth is real
When we play God
That's when we steal
The Blessing that come from his TRUTH

The Light you see is very real
If fear not faith is what you feel
You will cover your light time and again
And that TRUTH meant to be delivered by you
May never come through
For those who fear the presence they feel
For those who deny that GOD is real
And try hiding in the darkness
Rather than living in the Light
There is always hope
But help will not arrive
Until you ask for it

Led By The Spirit

A Verse for Cornelius

Some people will ask
Why YOU are the Chosen One
I ask…Why Not

We all have stories
That need to be told
Instead we hold them in silence
And tell ourselves
We can't change what already is
We have no impact on what will be
The fact is…Our reality
Is based on perception…Not the truth
Just because I step into the light
Doesn't make me an overnight success
I've been in dress rehearsal for years
Just ask the people you see with tears
In their eyes
They know the fears
I've overcome
The battles I've lost
And the cost THEY had to pay
To help me survive

Some people will ask
Why YOU are the Chosen One
I ask... Why Not

We've all got the same opportunity
To follow our dream
Find our purpose
If... like a salmon
You were born to swim upstream
But everyone tells you
You're Crazy
Will you choose to live a lie
Deny your true calling
And eventually die in vain
To sustain the illusion
Just to follow the crowd

Or will you stand tall... proud
And follow your heart
Will you have the courage
To answer God's call
Stand in the gap
Testify to all who will listen
The lessons
Learned by a Chosen One

Some people will ask
Why YOU are the Chosen One
I ask
WHY NOT

You can't find God
In a bottle or
Battle your demons
With money
Many say the right woman
Can save your soul
But that's just another way
Of selling out
No matter what you've been told
You can't find God
He's got to find YOU
Allow God to find YOU
And when you're Led By The Spirit
The true meaning of your life
Will be revealed
Healed from the inside out
All doubt will disappear
And you will fear
No more

Some people will ask
Why YOU are the Chosen One
I ask
WHY NOT

The miracle is not in being chosen
But in choosing to do the work
Temptations always lurk
In the shadows to challenge
Your faith
The Chosen
Fight for what they believe

African Angels

When you're Led By The Spirit
You can't conceive conceding
A battle already won
The Son of God
Died for our sins
And that's when he chose me
And YOU

Some people will ask
Why YOU are the Chosen One
I ask
WHY NOT

Faith

Poems of Faith

Is This All There Is

Is this it
Is this all there is
My life has no meaning
My days have no end
I search for my purpose
But it eludes me...What should I do

I ask for guidance
I pray for help
Only to find myself
Stumbling for answers
Struggling for sight
Hiding in the darkness
Rather than living in the light
My purpose eludes me. . .What should I do

This can't be it
This can't be all there is
My reality is a nightmare
And my nightmare won't end
I search for my purpose
THE THING I WAS BORN TO DO
Why it continues to elude me
I haven't got a clue

I'm looking outside myself
Afraid to look within

Is that why I feel lost
Why I'm stumbling for answers
Struggling for sight
Hiding in the darkness
Rather than living in the light

Look Inside
There you will find
The secrets of the universe
The reason you are here
God is waiting for you to sit still
Stop stumbling … Stop struggling
Allow God's Will
To be your guide

Believe

Matter and Energy
Spirit and Light
All combine to manifest
Your visions and dreams
In this world based on sight

Faith is the Angel
That transforms your desires
From a thought to reality
Simply because you believe
It has been said
Whatever you ask in my name,
You shall receive.

Blessings and miracles
Diamonds and pearls
Power and fame
All the wisdom of the world
Can be yours if you believe
What you cannot see
Spiritual energy in the name of the Master
Has always been the key
Hold to your faith
And you will become what you believe
Your thoughts grow as seeds
Even in a once barren soul

Don't forsake this blessing
Or one day you'll awake crumpled and old
From the weight of the world
Though for years you've been told
"Take your burdens to the Lord
And leave them there."
It's all about faith
Why would you choose pain, suffering, and despair.
When all you need to do is…
Believe

Trapped

*I was trapped
In my own personal hell
I couldn't be honest
With myself let alone
The people
The friends who wanted me
To tell them what was wrong
I called it being strong
Cutting myself off from
The people who cared
Dared to cross the abyss
And bring me back to reality
One by one
I sent them away
Then one day
I saw the flames
Everyone who came
Everyone I sent away
Was burning their bridge to me
Was I no longer worthy of their love
Was all hope lost
And the cost of dealing with me too high
I found myself trapped with no way out
The desperation
Fear and Frustration
Made me shout
I called on the name of the Lord*

And found comfort in his bosom
His loving arms
I was trapped
In my own personal hell
But the Lord brought me out
He bridged the abyss
And made me understand
Life is much too precious to miss
Don't isolate yourself
Don't burn your bridges to those who care
Put your faith in the Lord
No matter what you do
He will always be there

Having Faith

Having faith
Does not mean
You won't have challenges
Sorrow or pain
Only that the burden
Won't remain
On your shoulders
With angels to help lighten
Your load
Take it to Lord
And watch him explode
Your mountain
Into rocks that you
Can throw away

Having faith
Does not mean
You won't find yourself lost
That's a part of the test
The journey we all walk
As we define who we are
Find our star
To guide others along
Their way
Be not discouraged
Stay focused each and every day

Keenan Pendergrass

Having faith
Does not mean
There won't be times
When you are scared
But if you step out on a cloud anyway
You will find
Your life's calling
Is to testify by what
You do
And what you say

Step Out On Faith

Why is it so hard
To let go
When you know
That's exactly what you should do
Step out on faith
And hold on tight
No matter the storm
Day or night
No harm can come to you
An yet you hide
In your own shadow
Like there is something
You can do
Without the Lord
We are lost
We pay with our life
That's the cost
Of being vain
Contain your fear
Let go
Free fall
Remember it's the Lord
You should call
When faith is what you need

Keenan Pendergrass

Why is it so hard
To let go
When you know
That's exactly what you should do
Step out on faith

Your Purpose

Whatever it is that you
Were put on this earth to do
It lives
It breathes
It grows
Inside of you
No one will ever
Pull it out
Point it out
Shout eureka
Like they've struck gold
For you're the only one
Who can hold
God's blessing for you
It doesn't require a search
Hope, or even prayer
There's only one thing
You need do
Sit in silence and listen to your heart
Forget what people say
You can't do
Forget the fear
That wants to control you
Finding your purpose
Is an act of faith
Every success is a door
To your destiny

Never think that you're done
Never believe that you have just one
Purpose
Or you will miss the fun of being true to yourself
Whatever it is that you
Were put on this earth to do
It lives
It breathes
It grows
Inside of you
Listen to your heart
And you will know just what to do

Perfect Moments

Have you ever had a perfect moment that you recognized
As it occurred
As you purred inside your head
Amazed by the ease of the flow
The slow …slow…motion
That was the blessing
Of the blessing you received
So you could retrieve each second as if it were a day
Play the play
Again and again
Cause you always win in that perfect moment
That point in time when time does not exist
For you kissed the creator
Allowed him to enter your body
Your spirit
Your mind
You can't find what you already have
Control what you don't own
Greed is when you take more than you need
The credit belongs to God
Your perfect moment only ceases to exist
When you forget the kiss
The release
The perfect peace found inside the Creators arms
If you continue to trust
If you believe what you cannot see
Your perfect moment will last an eternity

Keenan Pendergrass

Give God all the credit
And your blessings will always flow from within
On clouds of light that feel like perfect moments
Frozen in time

Rainbows

I used to dream of rainbows
And nights lit by the moon
Day that smelled of honey suckle and lilac
And never ended too soon

I used to dream
Of these things and more
Of a world that was divine
But once I stepped into the streets of an unsaved world
I left my dreams behind

On the streets
My dreams seemed to fade away
My rainbow had no color
And clouds replaced the sun
That used to light each day

I was sad...Even depressed
I had no hope
And the best I could do
Was simply try to survive

Then one day someone said
My friend, you've got to dream
And believe with all your soul
You build your own rainbows
And each day is an opportunity to start

Don't let the chaos of an unsaved world
Drive a stake in your heart
You are the key to our salvation
We each are a part of the same spirit
The same energy flows through all our veins
Don't give our Adversary the reins
Don't give Evil an opportunity to grow
Remember your dream of rainbows
And nights lit by the moon
Days that smelled of honey suckle and lilac
And never ended too soon
Remember what it's like to have faith

Walk By Faith

When your direction is unclear
And you feel all alone
When darkness surrounds your path
And you can't find your way
Walk by Faith…Not by Sight

When everything seem to go wrong
And you feel your back is against the wall
When you make bad decisions
Thinking YOU can save the day
Walk by Faith…Not by Sight

Every day can't be perfect
Every choice won't be correct
Sometimes you have to go down
To appreciate going up
Walk by Faith…Not by Sight

All things are possible
When the Lord's purpose is clear
Nothing can stop your progress
When you are free of fear
Walk by Faith…Not by Sight

Honesty

Poems of Honesty

Searching

We walk around with the answers
searching questions that fit
Like life is a jeopardy quiz
And we have no choice but to sit
On the sidelines and watch

Our mission is often based in pride
With little direction
Why stop to decide
What we want
And who we want to be
As the situation plays out
We wait to see
What our role is
And how the story will end

Simply lost in a maze
Created in our own mind
We started the game
Now it's hard to find
A way to make it stop

What else can we do
Except walk around with the answers
Searching for questions that fit
Like life is a jeopardy quiz
And we have no choice but to sit

On the sidelines and watch

If you open your heart
Then open your eyes
Breathe with your soul
And remove your disguise
You might find the answers you seek
Life isn't a quiz that you win at all costs
You sold your soul once
That's how we got lost

We all have answers
With no questions in mind
But if we listen to our spirit
We can align with the universe
And start searching in a new way
Life is an act of faith
Not some game to play

Share Your Dream

Day after Day
We build on a dream
In our own little world
By a private little stream

And Day after Day
We build on a wall
Never building a net
In case we might fall

So Day after Day
As we build toward the sky
We see little else
Until life's passed us by

The day finally comes
When we attain our dream
In our own little world
With our own private stream

And on that day it becomes clear
We've been so caught up in fulfilling our dream
It's become the lonely life we were living
On the other side of the stream

Share Your Dream

Simple Beauty

We travel at the speed of sound
The speed of light
Running, rushing
Constantly pulled from left to right
No time to breathe
Less time to think
We live our lives standing on the brink
Wanting something more
Accepting nothing less
Than the world says we should be

For some it's chaos
For others it's bliss
But with each passing day
We tend to miss
The Simple Beauty
God puts in our path

A rainbow following an April shower
The colorful bloom of a spring flower
Kids playing tag right after school
A moonlit night, romantic and cool
Simple Beauty that we're too busy to see
Simple Beauty that is a part of God's amazing jubilee

God's beauty surrounds us
And his wisdom too

African Angels

Sometimes we move so fast
We miss the one clue
That would solve the puzzle
And set us free
Help us grow old like a majestic oak tree
Allow us to enjoy the blessings
Simply waking can provide
You see life is full of drama
Its speed can't always be denied
But sometimes we need to just stop and smell the roses
Enjoy life's Simple Beauty.

Your Power

Don't give away your power
It's the essence of your being
It's the light of your soul
Share it
But hold fast
Let no man cast
A spell that robs you of your essence
Or covers the light of your soul
You must be whole
To heal and feel the magic
This life can bring
Sing to the mountains high
And valley low
Sing as an angel
Beautiful and free
Celebrate this life
And the power you hold
Wealth untold in spirit and in true
Belongs to you
It's your gift
Cherish your power

We Run From The Truth

I open my heart
And reveal my soul
Without any fear
That my essence will be stolen
Or my spirit could be robbed
I fear not the truth
I struggle to comprehend.

While men will say they fear evil
They run from the truth
Unwavering
Unchanging
Perfect in its form
Still standing
Year after year
Able to endure
Storm after storm
The Truth
Is...
Was...
And Always Will Be...
THE SAME

It's a shame
All too often
We ignore the truth
And embrace

Keenan Pendergrass

What we can explain
Refrain from dealing with reality
Because while we fear evil
We run…
From THE TRUTH

Judgement Day

We all expect
The day will come
When the world will end
Until then
We pretend what we do
Matters not
It seems we forgot
Our teaching
On Judgement Day
The dead shall be raised
And then your misdeeds
Compared to your better days
So whether the world ends
While you're here
Or after you're gone
We will all see
The dawn
On the day
After the world ends
So spend more time
Living for today
Living the right way
Whatever that might mean
To you
'Cause the day after the world
Comes to an end
There won't be anything

Keenan Pendergrass

You can do
It will already be done

Why

Why put off for tomorrow
What you can do today

Why put off your problems
If you know they're not going away

Why run from yourself
When you know there's no place to hide

Why pretend you're happy
When sadness is only hidden by your pride
And the fear that things will only get worse

As you curse everything in sight
Others will delight in your pain
Cause misery loves company
And until you are strong enough
To go against the grain
Everything…
Will simply remain the same

Keenan Pendergrass

Better Days

There are so many blessings
That simply go unclaimed
People seem to be scared
That somehow their blessings
Will be drained
And somehow not refilled

But if that's true
If blessings are like time
You get to start over fresh
Each and every day
You're given more than enough blessings
To help you on your journey
To find the peace of God
And the joy you hold inside
Pride may keep you from opening
The door that holds your promise yet fulfilled

Just know you can't stockpile your blessings
Like milk once spoiled or spilled
There's no turning back the hands of time
What's done is done
And simply put
No one's won a thing
Everyday blessings go unclaimed
Because we fear our own success
And unless we change our ways

We will always hope for Better Days
Never realizing they're already here.

Know Your Soul

Sometimes illusions can be a guide
But all to often they only hide behind
The secrets of the truth
Illusions you see are all too real
Because they hinge on what you feel
Not what is true
If I only tell you what I want you to know
If I only tell you what I can see
With that truth you must go out into the world
My illusion becomes your reality
And so the seed becomes a tree
That's fed by the illusion of your new reality
Illusions and reality go hand in hand
Separated only by time...Grains of sand
And until you understand the higher truth
Reality and illusion are essentially the same
Only your spirit is able to tame
The beast raging out of control
Hold to the truth that is in your heart
No matter what you see with your eyes
For life is a series of illusions disguised as reality
That serve to test your faith
Know your soul
And you will know the truth

I Wonder

Sometimes I wonder
How much I've really grown
My friends all say I've changed
But is that good or bad
What happened to the tolerance...
The patience I once had
For the people I used to call my friends

Have I really grown
If I no longer have time
For the problems I used to own
I see them in you
And simply walk away
When I should accept you where you are
And not judge you for holding your miracles at bay
By your words and deeds
We all lead by example
And when there's ample proof you've grown
Selfish not wiser
Callus not caring
Judging not forgiving
You're living a lie

If I have no patience for you
But expect you to tolerate me
I must be like the man in the bible
Who had eyes but could not see

Keenan Pendergrass

The connection that exists
Is simple to understand
There is only one bridge
Between me and my fellow man
And that is God

Sometimes I wonder
How much I've really grown
My friends all say I've changed
But is that good or bad
What happened to the tolerance…
The patience I once had
For the people I used to call my friends

Understanding

Poems of Understanding

God's Garden

A gardener prunes
his plants so they might grow
He cuts them carefully, precisely,
So their flowers can bloom
He clears the weeds and tends the soil
So all the world can see
The beauty that is within
…The Creator's majesty.
And so it is with people
Like plants we too must grow
God prunes us with challenges
Trials and tribulations we often think unfair
Disasters that might beg the question…
Does God really care
It starts to make sense
When our bloom reaches the light
We needed God's challenge to grow
And for all that is lost
we gain so much more
Once you know love
No one can ever close that door
Once you know peace
There's a serenity you start to feel
Once you know GOD
You find faith is your shield
And you can stand proudly
Proclaiming that he's real

Not because you read it
or heard it second hand
We know God is real through our trials
And now we understand.
The Secret of God's Garden
Is the strength we find in times of pain
For only we can make our blossoms grow
And it's up to us to let our children know
The hurt we endure when we feel the pain
Show's the world how much we gain
From the love, the peace, the warmth
And yes, the pruning found
In God's Garden

How can I be GOD

I can't turn water into wine
And no one will ever call me divine
I can't even find my place on this earth
Who I'm supposed to be
And now you want me to believe
Your religious fantasy

How can I be GOD

I need glasses to see
And who in their right mind would follow me
Certainly no one trying to set their spirit free
In this world full of sin
I'm lost just like you
And now you want me to believe
What you say is true

How can I be GOD
How can I be GOD
How can GOD be ME

Or my mother
Or my sister
Or THAT man across the street....
Or my minister
Or my teacher
Or the Good Samaritan who...

Keenan Pendergrass

helped me get back on my feet...

CAN THEY BE GOD
ARE THEY GOD
AM I

The Trinity

And in an instant it all made sense
I had heard the same words
Time and again but this time
This time
It was different; it was clear
I guess the words cut though my fear
They supported me
Comforted me
Enlightened me
They fed me…

YOU ARE GOD
YOU MAKE THE TRINITY COMPLETE
And in an instant it all made sense

GOD The Father protects you
He has since time began
GOD The Son gave his life for you
Forgiving the sins of Adam
When we were ban from the Garden

And The HOLY SPIRIT lives inside of you
As a part of the Master's plan

YOU ARE GOD
YOU MAKE THE TRINITY COMPLETE

And in an instant it all made sense
I had heard the same words
Time and again but this time
This time
It was different; it was clear
I guess the words cut though my fear
They supported me
Comforted me
Enlightened me
They fed me…
YOU ARE A PART OF THE ONE*SONG
THE UNI*VERSE

YOU ARE GOD

The Door is Open

There is a darkness that hides
The mystery of my promise
The God given talents
That make me unique
The door is open
But light will not exist
Until I enter the darkness
To discover what twist
Of fate awaits me…

And there in is my dilemma
There in is my hesitation

My destiny has arrived
Time and again yet I fear
I have not prepared for what
God wants me to do
My faith is wavering
Thought I say it's my foundation
I must believe before
I can see
The light that encircles me
Like a cocoon…
Nurturing…
Protecting…
Fleeting…

And there in is my dilemma
There in is my hesitation

I must surrender to my fear
I must trust the thing
That awaits me
Good or bad
Knowing it is my destiny
I cannot run from myself
But I can hide in the darkness
Along with the mystery of my promise
The God given talents
That make me unique

And there in is my dilemma
There in is my hesitation

I have seen the light
And it is me
I cannot run
I cannot see
I am blinded by faith
Yet frozen in time
My hesitation must end
For it is itself a crime

I am cheating myself
And trying to cheat God
How arrogant I am
How stupid can I be
I keep going 'round the same circle
Fooling no one but me

I create my on dilemmas
Therefore I can cease
The drama that surrounds me
And find internal peace
The hesitation will end
And the energy will flow
To the God given talents
That make me unique

The door is open
But light will not exist
Until I enter to discover
What twist of fate awaits me
For I am the light

The Spirit

The Spirit gives life
to the trees
the leaves
The flowers
that tower over
grass glistening with morning's dew

The Spirit is the beauty
in the rain
and snow capped terrain
the eagles
that soar over lakes and rivers
with their own private view

The Spirit speaks to
your heart
your mind
body and soul
Whispering in your ear
Reminding you of things
You weren't aware that you knew

The Spirit is your guide
Through the maze we call Earth
From Birth to Re-Birth
From dusk to dawn
When we step into the light

African Angels

We are finally able to see
That we are
THE SPIRIT
It's in the trees
The leaves
The flowers that tower over
Grass glistening with mornings dew

It's The Spirit
You're The Spirit
We're The Spirit
And The Spirit IS GOD

So That You Can Fly

Who knows why
No one can really tell
The purpose of another
His point for being here
But if you've been touched
If you held his Spirit near
You were blessed by GOD above
Love is the only thing that's real
Everything else is an attempt to steal...
Your joy
Destroy the light
That shines within
It matters not
What you've done
Where you've been
Why you've run
What made you cry
Life's challenges and lessons
Are really air under your wings
. . .So that you can fly
They don't have to make sense
And there's only one reason why
They seem so hard and often unfair . . .
They are there so that you can fly
Don't deny
Your ability to soar
You'll find your spirit

African Angels

And so much more
Our purpose in life
Might not always be clear
And we may not understand
The challenges of those we hold dear
But the next time you want to cry
Remember
God gives each of us challenge
...So that we can fly

Flowing

Feel the universe
Flowing through your veins
Its energy is your life source
The same life force that radiates
From the sun
Causes flowers to bloom
And rivers to run
Like children playing
In a field
The universe contains
All knowledge and power
And it's available to you
Delight in the journey
Before you
The challenge
The lesson designed to reveal
The knowledge you hold inside
Most people hide
Their head in shame
They fear the game
Can never be won
They don't realize the same energy
That radiates from the sun
Is also at their core
Just waiting to be tapped
They feel trapped
Instead they should

African Angels

Feel the universe
Flowing through their veins
Its energy is your life source
The same life force that radiates
From the sun
Causes flowers to bloom
And rivers to run
Like children playing
In a field

Comprehension

Does a fish
Comprehend water
Does a bird
Comprehend air
Does man
Comprehend God
Or simply expect him
To always be there
Watching, waiting, nurturing, protecting
While we're neglecting
Our responsibilities
Here on earth
How much is your life really worth
If you can throw it away
Day by day
Hour by hour
Ignoring the rain showers
The hail storms
Ignoring warning signs
In any form
But what will you do
In your last hour
That day when you're caught
In the meteor shower
We can't dismiss
One day there WILL be a meteor shower
And whatever you call bliss

African Angels

Will disappear
In it's place will be
Your worst fear
Unless you're protected by God's Grace
Does a fish
Comprehend water
Does a bird
Comprehend air
Does man
Comprehend God
Or simply expect him
To always be there

Keenan Pendergrass

Observations From A Parallel Universe

There is a veil that separates
You from reality
Keeps the totality of all that is
From hitting you with it's full force
But we're on a collision course with destiny
And some among you are privileged to see
What's on the other side
To feel the experience
Then share the evidence of a higher power
Relate what is
In word and deed
Provide observations from a parallel universe
And allow you to get a glimpse of the beauty
Contained in the flower of your seed
Understand the purpose of the challenges...the tests
That hold our blessings
And provide the key to the door
Leading to our next opportunity to grow
Study the word and you too will come to know
The secrets of the universe
On the other side of the veil
The parallel universe of your soul

The Best Thing You Ever Knew

If the worst thing that ever happened to you
Gave birth to the best thing you ever knew
Would it be worth the pain
Would your loss
Be off set by your gain
Or would you miss your blessing
Addressing the reasons why

We all deny
The role we play is our own pain
Until we're alone
When like a familiar refrain in a song we can't forget
We see the scene in our head again and again
It's not going to end until you understand
The moment at hand

The worst that ever happened to you
Just gave birth to the best thing you ever knew

Had it not been for that one moment in time
When everything fell apart
You'd still be lost
Instead you crossed the abyss and found your way
Day by day you climbed out of the hole
You thought was a mountain peak
Unique
Only in the sense that it's yours

Keenan Pendergrass

Scores of holes are dug each and every day
Hiding the mountain thought to reach so high
But you will never touch the sky
By chasing the infinite reasons why this thing
Had to happen to you
Accept it
Own it
Embrace it as the blessing that it is
And the worst that ever happens to you
Will give birth to the best thing you ever knew

The Universe

You created the Universe
The Universe didn't create you
True to form
I only have to look into your eyes
To see God
His Spirit gives you life
And me Hope
Yet everyday I grope in the darkness
Trying to get a grasp on a reality
No two people will see as the same
Until they suspend all they know to be
Or perceive not to be
Free your mind
And the blessings will follow
Trust your heart
And you will know
You created the Universe
The Universe didn't create you